CW01619938

9 8 7 6 5 4 3 2 1 0

First published 2023

Bible references are from a wide range of translations.

ISBN 978-1-9161729-6-8

All enquires to jbugden@hotmail.co.uk

Cover design and Typesetting by Angela Selfe
Cover background image by www.freepik.com

Printed in the UK

RECALIBRATE

REALITY:
Dismantling old mindsets, cultures, habits, and practices in order to engage with God's reset

CLARITY:
Clearing the fog and decluttering from the conventional to facilitate revelation and momentum

Jonathan Bugden

Published by
spirit level communications

Part 1

REALITY

Dismantling old mindsets, cultures, habits,
and practices in order to engage with God's reset.

Many people forego encounters with God because they settle for theological certitude.

Contents

Introduction

I have been urged to write this material as a way of bringing greater freedom to more people, as they realise the need to 'break out' from the box they have been stuck in. I try to write humbly, simply, and lovingly, more than rationally, critically, or with academic prowess. The deep joy I have found in the 'new', along with many others I know, is motivation enough to write and to encourage you to read this book.

If you are unaware of the pivotal moment in history in which we are living, along with the seismic change God has initiated, the contents may be puzzling and perhaps seem somewhat irrelevant – but I challenge you to open yourself up to God at this vital time and let Him show you what He wants to.

However, if God has already stirred your heart, stimulated your spirit, and renewed your mind, I hope this will bring some clarity, navigational advice and, most of all, a passion to ask Holy Spirit for further insight and wisdom to discover more of what God is doing. For the doctrinally obsessed, this is a different way of exploring what the outworking of 'sanctification' looks like. As spiritual beings in human bodies, we live in two realities – physical and spiritual. Our personal 'reality' is determined by the extent to which we live in one or other of these.

If physical reality, along with thoughts, emotions, and current circumstances loom largest for us, then the spiritual will have to take a back seat. Conversely, if we look at the physical from a spiritual reality, we will interact with it differently.

When one of these realities is our 'foreground' the other will recede to the 'background'.

Which reality is the dominant one for you? Remember that none of us is perfect and we're all on a journey of development – don't be despondent, be hungry!

Many believers find themselves 'stuck', like a beached boat, a broken-down car or a climber on a sheer rock face. This is a moment in time to allow a rescue or recovery to happen, and Holy Spirit is a genius at both! The only thing He needs from us is our permission and co-operation.

I have a favour to ask you, the reader; please don't apply what you read to someone else or to the 'church', **it's written for you!**

My prayer is that you discover your own personal revelation as you dialogue with Holy Spirit.

On the left-hand page of each chapter is the 'problem' that needs addressing, and on the right-hand page is the expression of the new that is released when that issue is dismantled. We are all travelling from 'left' to 'right'.

With love,
Jonathan

Belief without encounter

It is perfectly possible to believe that you have a connection and relationship with God that is real when actually it's something of an illusion. Many who have a belief in God and claim to be Christians are really adherents of the Christian religion who have signed up to a belief system and have faith in it; they strive to do the 'right' thing, they keep the rules, and they rarely miss a church meeting.

Startlingly, this is no guarantee of an authentic, dynamic relational connection to Father, Jesus, and Holy Spirit. There is the appearance of a godly life on the outside, there is an intellectual conviction of what they believe, and regular Christian activity. However, the only question that matters is how genuine, vibrant, and current your personal relationship with God is. Encounter that is restricted by belief leads to delusion. Do you know about God or intimately 'know' God?

Learning about someone and being in a love relationship with them are two very different things. This was exemplified by the Pharisees, who knew everything about God but missed Jesus and a life-giving encounter with him. Experience was missed because knowledge was given greater importance.

Notes ....

....

....

....

....

....

Vibrant relational life

Once a person has tasted the real thing, anything else will be disappointing, dull, and hard work. Once you have an encounter with God you won't settle for anything less. It ruins you – in a good way! Healthy relationships always mature, develop, and bring fulfilment to the parties involved. So it is with our ever-deepening connectedness with God. It's a romance that excites, brings laughter, and makes the heart beat faster. There are shared secrets, and there is gazing into each other's eyes, and a deep togetherness. If you are not finding joy, peace, and fulfilment in your relationship with Father, Jesus, and Holy Spirit, something is amiss, and it saddens Them because there is so much more that they have that they want to reveal to you. Don't settle for less than is in the heart of God for you his child and friend. Break free from what restrains you and restricts God. There is an incredible discovery to be made on this journey as repeated encounters lead to 'entwinement'; it moves from an occasional 'mountain top' experience to regular interaction.

Notes ....

....

....

....

....

....

....

....

Control and hierarchy

Throughout history people have sought to control other people, whether nations or employees or families or congregations. Sadly, this drive/desire is not healthy, does not honour God, and ruins the lives of many – as history attests. Let's urgently begin to outlaw this practice wherever we find it, to gently call it out when we discern it, and refuse to indulge in it ourselves. The place in which this abhorrent behaviour should be least apparent is surely amongst the people of God – but it may well be where it is most widely found. Leadership was never meant to be hierarchical, dictatorial, coercive, or manipulative. Again, this is especially true in the context of church, yet it is arguably the place where it is most widely observable and unchecked. The level of collateral damage or the 'drop out' rate as a result of leaders exercising this kind of power is staggering; it stretches back over centuries. The abuse of spiritual power and position is devastating, damaging, and destructive – always. As part of the current 'reset' that God has initiated, there is a call to eradicate this expression of leadership.

Notes ....

....

....

....

....

....

....

Freedom, release, and empowerment

As we transition from the 'old' to the 'now', there are things we need to discover. As we intentionally abandon previous ways of controlling other people, whether we are leaders or not, we discover that there is a better way, a God-honouring way, and Holy Spirit is the perfect mentor, guide, coach, and friend to help us on this journey of discovery (thankfully). There is such harmony, mutual honour, and love within the Trinity between Father, Jesus, and Holy Spirit, with no trace of jostling, competition, or control. Union and peace without hierarchy! What an amazing model, for those who follow and represent God, of how to relate, think, and behave. There is such joy in seeing other people flourish, mature, excel, and fly free that you can't explain until you've experienced it! Empowering and releasing people to be the best version of the person God created them to be is so liberating and fulfilling both for them and for you. I understand that some people regard this as utopian and unrealistic, but I have proof in my own life and other people's lives that this is not only desirable but achievable. If the power of God is in us and we don't limit it, then why would we not expect to access and enjoy this glorious freedom and release?

Notes ....

....

....

....

....

Analysis paralysis

One of the biggest 'hoodwinks' ever to establish itself amongst Christians is the deception that our faith is primarily something that occurs on an intellectual level. This is particularly true of the Western world and its conviction that we must always be rational, logical, and reasonable. However, this error relegates the whole gamut of spiritual experience to something that is untrustworthy and unreliable, and for many believers this has promoted theology and doctrinal correctness (whatever that is!) to a place of pre-eminence; here the person of god is everything as opposed to a belief system about him. It's such a restrictive and misguided position to adopt. This need to have a defined and finalised set of beliefs usually prevents a person from exploring and discovering the mysteries, secrets, and experiences of God. God's spirit to our spirit is the primary form of communication between us, not intellectually grasping a truth. Sad or what? If faith is based in a creed, we become frozen and trapped in it and lose sight of the life and relationship that Jesus offers us, which lies beyond our cognitive capacity.

Many have talked about not putting God in a box but then fallen prey to a mental inflexibility that results in them doing that very same thing!

Notes ....

....

....

....

Personal revelation

Revelation that is only through other people is at best second hand and at worst something that can trap us and lead us to erroneously conclude we 'know' something we don't. Whilst we recognize the gifts and ministries of others, it's essential that we receive personal revelation from God for ourselves, not least because it has more power, purity, and integrity. God's desire to reveal, communicate, and envision applies to every one of His children – not just a 'specialist' few. Now, more than ever, this is the day of the 'priesthood of all believers' – the good news is that this includes you. Jesus has done away with the need for us to have those who can mediate with God on our behalf, and Father has provided Holy Spirit to show us all that we need to understand and discover. By faith, just like you did for salvation, reach out and take what Jesus is offering you – interaction with the divine. **It's a life of excitement, mystery, peace, freedom, and joy, which you really don't want to miss out on!** Wisdom means we 'weigh' what we receive, but so many assume God has nothing to say to them, they "don't hear God like others", but God is sharing things with us all the time – the issue is our awareness.

Notes ....

....

....

....

....

....

Fear, risk aversion, and passivity

It's stating the obvious to say that some people are more adventurous than others. However, much of our 'playing it safe', cautious approach finds its roots in fear.

Fear of getting it wrong or being ridiculed or overruled.

Being a disciple of Jesus will inevitably offer us the option to be courageous and 'step out' in faith. Faith and aversion to risk are not compatible with one another. One way or the other, one will always affect and dominate the other! Fear has been, and remains, a major cause of inertia, anxiety, and opting out of God-ordained assignments by believers. Yet one of the most common exhortations in the Bible is, 'Do not be afraid' (not least because we have not been given a spirit of fear and timidity), yet many are bound by fear. What causes fear in you?

Not recognising who we are 'in Jesus' will make us overly cautious and overly sensitive to criticism, both of which are paralysing.

How have we got to this place where we lack the courage to live as Jesus intended?

We are called to be a voice not an echo, and to fulfil our unique destiny from our unique identity and character. You don't have to be loud or pushy, just brave, and trusting of the voice and nudges of Holy Spirit.

Notes ....

....

....

Adventure and assignment

Breaking free from a place and mindset of fear, caution, and passivity is the doorway to a whole new life of discovery, excitement, and fulfilment.

In any relationship, as time goes by, trust develops, and both parties feel increasingly secure in each other. Out of our deepening relationship with God, we can find a love and trust that combats fear and 'people pleasing', which in turns leads to a place of confidence, assurance, and faith. This foundation facilitates us to launch out into adventure and assignments, to find our purpose with excitement rather than dread. Living out of our God-given identity to fulfil our God-given destiny is a life of fun, faith, joy, and impact.

Our willingness to embrace the adventures God has planned for us, rather than dodge or ignore them, leads to the abundant life that is the inheritance that Jesus promised us. It truly is more amazing than you can imagine. Failure isn't wrong - we often learn and grow through it. This is not dependent on whether we are an introvert or an extrovert but whether we are willing or not. Everything that is needed is found in Jesus and facilitated by Holy Spirit.

It's over to you!

Notes ....

....

....

....

Malnourished spirit

Most people invest significant time and effort in themselves to develop a healthy body and mind from birth to adulthood. Many adults then continue to invest in education, career, health, skills, and leisure. This, of course, is not wrong but is indeed to be encouraged as a responsible and fulfilling way to live a full life.

However, astonishingly, the most important part of us is largely ignored and so remains underdeveloped and without much of a voice. This vital part is our **spirit**.

A shrivelled, prune-like spirit is the very antithesis of what our Creator intended. It is our spirit which carries the eternal part of us that will never die; it's where the divine DNA resides, and it's from there that we can discover who we were created to be and what our God-intended purpose is. Many have made the spirit subservient to the mind or to feelings, which results in a life that functions out of kilter with its original design.

How bizarre, neglectful, even stupid that anyone would relegate their spirit to a minor role in their existence. It is difficult to have an 'eternal perspective' on life with a muted spirit.

How much attention do you pay to the health of your spirit and what is occurring in it?

Notes ....

....

....

....

....

Mature spirit

It's important not to link spirit maturity with cerebral knowledge. The extent of our mental knowledge has very little to do with the degree of maturity of our spirit – in fact, it often mitigates against it. Information makes us more knowledgeable for sure, but head knowledge and spirit reality are completely different things.

It's vital that we do not confuse them, as that can easily create the illusion of relational reality when all we have is information. We must divorce reputation, status, ministerial experience, and doctrinal expertise from a mature spirit.

What characterises a mature spirit?

> 'Mature believers respond only to the impulses of Holy Spirit.' (John 9:23)

> 'Abundant fruit (*note fruit not gifts*) demonstrates mature disciples.' (John 15:8)

> 'Love is the mark of true maturity.' (Col 3:14)

> 'The mature are recognised as those who don't live to please themselves and are patient with the immature.' (Romans 15:1)

Wisdom, humility, self-control, kindness, gentleness, meekness, and contentment are on show when there is a mature spirit.

Notes ....

....

....

Lack of identity

It is so sad when believers are oblivious to who God says we are. Every person is created with a unique character, personality, identity, and destiny as determined and chosen by the Creator himself. Not being aware of that will lead to a sense of lostness, insignificance, or hopelessness – puzzled and perplexed as to what life is all about. Pardon the mundane analogy, but if a sieve is designed to strain water, it is bizarre to try to use it to drink coffee from. It is not suitable, designed, or appropriate for anything other than its one purpose. Being ignorant of our identity, as designed by God, is debilitating and will mean we are largely unaware of our purpose or our assignments on earth. Heartbreakingly, many folks progress through life and 'become' someone they were not designed to be, resulting in an inner feeling of frustration and unfulfilment.

We are not to be defined by what we do but rather who we are. Career, relationships, and experiences all shape us, but our identity is not to be lost – they affect us but shouldn't define us – God has already done that.

I recommend you take time out to ask Holy Spirit for His input on this matter – it will likely differ from yours!

Notes ....

....

....

....

Security and assurance

Relationship with God enables us to fully comprehend who He made us to be and why He chose us to live at this time in human history. When this is our reality, we discover a level of personal fulfilment, security (mental, emotional, and spiritual), and an assurance that we didn't previously realise were possible. It's so extraordinary and breathes life and revelation into a lot of scripture verses! When we become spiritually (different from intellectually or theologically) aware that Holy Spirit is residing in our spirit there is overwhelming inner peace, serenity and 'knowing' that is stronger than our circumstance, feelings, or experiences of life.

> 'Confidence and strength flood the hearts of the lovers of God who live in awe of Him.' (Proverbs 14:26)

> 'I leave the gift of peace with you – My peace. Not the fragile kind of peace, but My perfect peace.' (John 14:27)

> 'My confidence in my identity in Christ enables me to overcome every difficulty, for I have an intimate revelation of God.'
> (2 Tim 1:2)

Notes ....

....

....

....

Orphan heart

If we lack, or have lost, an awareness of who God says we are as followers of Jesus, there is a strong possibility that we will succumb to a sense of feeling like an orphan. Many believers live under a cloud of perceiving themselves as useless, ineffective, insignificant, abandoned, and forgotten. I'm so saddened by meeting people in this state of mind because it's not God's heart for any of his children and what's more, **it's untrue!**

Often, it's life experiences and abuse by other people that leads to this horrid conclusion and despair. For some it began even before birth or in early childhood; for others it was in a church (makes me shudder), and for others in tragedy or loss in adult life.

An orphan is not in relationship with their parents (even if they have knowledge of them) and so is not a recipient of their love and care.

A believer who is not an experiential receiver of Father God's love, care, tenderness, and reassurance will struggle not to feel bereft and sad.

Many poor choices, wrong perceptions, and ungodly beliefs stem from being orphan-hearted. It creates a distorted view of God, of ourselves, and of our world.

Notes ....

....

....

....

....

Abba and sonship

Feeling like a spiritual orphan is so sad, not least because it's the very opposite of what is God's heart and desire for His children. If we don't experience God as our loving, gentle, kind heavenly father then we won't experience what it feels like to know we are His child. **It's a spirit thing not a head thing.**

The joy, peace, comfort, and wellbeing that come from encountering Him as our father are indescribable, healing, life-changing, and transformative – really!!

We know that He wants us to be constantly connected to Him as our Abba – Daddy.

Pause and think about that and what it means for you. When we experientially know God as our father, we can start to enjoy the joys and benefits of being his child. Jesus promised:

> 'I will never leave you helpless or abandon you as orphans.'
>
> (John 14:18)

> 'Every spiritual blessing in the heavenly realm has already been lavished upon you as a gift from our wonderful heavenly Abba.'
>
> (Eph 1:3)

Are you living from the reality of being a 'son' (please note this is a gender-blind term) or an orphan?

Notes ....

....

....

Performance orientation

We live in a society that is obsessed with success, fame, and a celebrity culture. In almost every area of life, people are 'measured', graded, and labelled to determine how 'successful' they are.

What accreditation, recognition, or achievement has been obtained often decides whether a person is worth knowing or not. This mindset has permeated people's thinking and attitudes to the point where someone's real value is overlooked, despised, or ignored.

This value system is so engrained in our thinking that many have become unaware that they use it.

It's a great time to ask Holy Spirit:

'Am I performance driven?'

'How does it affect my perception of myself and of other people?'

This 'performance' perspective of judging ourselves and others has, tragically, penetrated church life and structure too. The way we measure the 'value' of a person is flawed to the point of being very Christlike. This needs urgently addressing, both individually and collectively, if we are to find the glorious alternative that has always been in God's heart. Our value is in who we were created to be more than in what we 'achieve'.

Notes ....

....

....

....

....

....

Acceptance and destiny

When we lose the need to 'perform' for people's approval or acceptance, we can experience the joy of knowing we are the apple of our Father's eye. He speaks over us as He did over Jesus 'this is my beloved one in whom I delight'. Wow!

What relief, release, and rejoicing flow from that, followed by freedom from constantly 'trying', and from people pleasing. You are changed forever by this breakthrough; it's life transforming. It is where rest, contentment, peace, and acceptance are found.

From this place of acceptance and contentment, we can begin to discover both our God-given identity and our God-designated assignment on earth. Nobody needs to go through life not knowing why they are here. Our arrival was God's timing, our character is God's design, and our purpose is God's plan. The only thing we are asked to do is to collaborate and co-operate with Him to see them manifest. Revelling in the reality of our acceptance by Father will also allow us to stop wrongly evaluating and judging other people.

Our ministry of reconciliation, along with authentic unity, will finally have a chance to flourish, especially amongst believers.

Notes ....

....

....

....

....

....

Harsh and critical judgement

I have been aghast and heartbroken over the last five decades by one thing more than most others, and that is the venomous, critical, harsh, judgemental way in which Christians speak about, and to, one other.

The great irony of this is that Jesus explained it was our love for one another in His family that would be appealing to unbelievers and draw them to Him.

I'm not really sure how we, as His children, could have got this more wrong than we have, are you?

Believing that God wants us to defend His 'truth' rather than display His heart has led many to the erroneous idea that it is ok to be critical towards those who disagree with our interpretations and theological opinions. Our 'right' to correct the thinking of others has become so engrained in us that we are oblivious to any tendency we have to be harshly judgemental.

Given that God is presented by Jesus as the essence of love, it seems bizarre that Christendom has become riddled with conditional love, pride, and 'speaking ill' of others.

It is surely time to allow Holy Spirit to eradicate this way of being in order to liberate us to represent God to the world with authenticity.

Notes ....

....

....

....

Love and kindness

When the filter that causes us to see with a critical spirit is dissolved, an amazing development occurs that frees us to be a truer likeness of Jesus in the way we think and behave. This doesn't require us to strain and strive to 'try harder', to make more effort, or to do penance! Instead, by the simple act of staying close to Him we start to become more loving – even if it's little by little. It is in our spirit to be kind and loving (created in His image remember), but our body and soul can drown our spirit out. It is appealing to people when they encounter a loving, kind, and gentle person. Jesus was just such a person, and as his followers we're called to be the same and imitate Him. It's not complicated!

> 'My parting word to you is: Love one another deeply.'
> (John 15:17)

> 'Live in harmony with one another and demonstrate love, sympathy and kindness towards each other.' (1 Peter 3:8)

> 'If He loved us with such tremendous love, then loving one another should be our way of life.' (1 John 4:11)

Notes ....

....

....

....

....

Certitude

For many years (centuries in fact) Christians have espoused the virtue of being certain about what to believe. Theological bedrocks, doctrinal convictions, and scriptural interpretation need to be fixed, immovable, and unshakeable, we were told. Indeed, I taught this to others myself some years ago.

However, there are some dangerous fundamental flaws in this opinion and approach (in my humble opinion).

Having everything doctrinally 'sorted':

- ➢ can make us deaf and blind to fresh revelation,
- ➢ can easily lead to spiritual arrogance,
- ➢ makes the mind our final arbiter when God designed our spirit to have that role,
- ➢ assumes that the 'interpretation' we have chosen is the right one.

The best example in the Bible of this fixed stance is the Pharisees – who were the experts and the official representatives of God (interesting contrast to the disciples).

I had to acknowledge that there was more of the 'religious' in myself than I cared to admit, and I strongly urge you to allow Holy Spirit surgery to remove it for you too (aka a Pharisectomy).

Notes ....

....

....

Mystery and loose ends

Relying on a spirit-to-Spirit connection with God is much safer and more enjoyable than relying on a set of beliefs based on a book. If God is God, and we are not, then there are surely going to be things we don't and can't understand or explain. Mystery is inevitable in our connection with Father, Jesus, and Holy Spirit unless we set boundaries that preclude it. We can't hope to reduce God to a size we can handle – although many still fruitlessly try. The 'not knowing' isn't an issue for those who are relationally entwined with the Lord – they feel secure in their spirit and so they're neither frustrated nor agitated.

It's many years since Holy Spirit clearly explained to me that if I wanted a deeper relationship, I would need to be content to live with loose ends in my life. That has immensely helped me in more recent times.

Our spirits can accommodate mystery (as well as many other things) in a way our mind cannot, so check who is in charge!

Ask Holy Spirit to help you find peace and contentment in the not knowing. What boundaries need to be removed?

Notes ....

....

....

....

....

....

Second-hand revelation

Anything that God didn't reveal to you personally is second-hand revelation.

Pause and consider that for a while . . .

This, of course, does not mean that we ignore everything anyone else says, but we are to carefully check it out with Holy Spirit before taking it onboard. Many of the secrets, mysteries, and 'hidden' things of God are made known in private rather than during platform preaching. Such a lot of people hear a great teaching which came to the teacher by revelation and then 'adopt' it as their own. However, unless and until that becomes your personal reality, it's only theoretical, not experiential. For example, I have heard leaders speak passionately about the Father heart of God and urge people to receive that truth, but it's clear they are not living in the reality of that love themselves. This leads to the perpetuation of unreality, illusion, and even hypocrisy.

Believing that God 'doesn't' reveal things to me like He does others is an ungodly belief and untrue, but it explains why we prefer being 'spoon-fed' by other people.

Ask Holy Spirit to show you what you believe that is theory rather than reality.

Notes ....

....

....

....

....

Personal, authentic reality

Never was there a more important time to understand 'the priesthood of all believers' than now. Holy Spirit is beside you constantly, Father is pouring His love over you, and Jesus is calling you to intimacy with Him.

Be still and 'know' the fullness of the Godhead – just you and them! Let's say things as they really are, let's be honest about what's real and what's not. Let's stop pretending we know God better than we do. Let's cease trying to impress others with our spiritual credentials.

Let's destroy the lie that God only communicates with an anointed few!

The enemy hates authenticity so much because it's a key to finding new depths in our relationship with the Trinity.

Please understand that I'm not discounting or devaluing the spiritual gifts that God gives to people, but each of us needs to hear from God on a **one-to-one** basis first. Recall and review the things that God has shown you personally (as opposed to through others).

What do you deduce from this?

Ask Holy Spirit for the wisdom to discern what needs to happen next and the faith to move forward with it.

Notes ....

....

....

....

Hurried and over-busy

We live in a world that is fast-paced, driven, and 'instant'. This makes it difficult for people to eliminate hurry, haste, and hassle. It's a case of having to go against the tide with determination, perseverance, and a willingness to be misunderstood. One big problem with this speed of living is that it is at odds with our Creator and his design of us.

It's easy to mistake being over-busy as a sign of our success, how much we are achieving, productivity, and how well we are 'serving' God. Sadly, it's unlikely to be a true measure. It's hard to be wise, kind, and considerate when we are always in a hurry. We tend not to give others the time or attention that they deserve, we make rash decisions, and put ourselves at a high risk of burnout. Why would anyone live like this when there is a better way?

How much of a hurry are you living your life in?

....

How can you become ruthless in eliminating that hurry?

....

This choice is fundamental to our spiritual and physical wellbeing. Let's follow our Maker's design!

Notes ....

....

....

Rest and discernment

Living in a hurry mitigates against discovering how to be still, how to benefit from rest, and how to live in peace. Slowing our internal rhythm, synchronising our pace with Holy Spirit, and listening before we speak will all make for a more enjoyable life, a more meaningful relationship with God, and a better version of ourselves for others to encounter.

The Bible is crammed with exhortations, teachings, and wisdom about the secret and benefits of being still, of sabbath rest, and of 'sitting' with God. Even the mysteries, secrets, and keys of heaven are to be discovered in the secret place. Do you regularly experience the peace and joy that's found in the quiet place with God?

....

When there is this stillness in our rested spirit, it's amazing how insight, wisdom, and discernment appear – it's a supernatural and extraordinary outcome of rest. It removes so much 'striving' to be more godly, anointed, and holy. When we are living from this place, these things flourish without our effort and graft.

Notes ....

....

....

....

....

....

....

Despair and hopelessness

Anyone in an authentic relationship with God need not be overwhelmed by despair and a lack of hope when they encounter them. Life throws up situations and events that can be tough, even catastrophic, and our emotions and thoughts struggle, but with God's presence within us, all is not lost. The world we live in has many who, sadly, though understandably, lose hope or give up on life. Part of the 'good news' of Jesus is that He brings hope, even in hopeless circumstances. There are also folk (including not a few Christians) who feel life is unfulfilling and disappointing and their hope diminishes. These are powerful emotions, but it's not God's heart, plan, or design that we would be overcome by them.

Are you struggling with feeling like this?

....

Are people you know trapped in a scenario of lost hope?

....

Are there situations where you could help to restore hope?

....

What solution/counsel does Holy Spirit show you?

....

....

Notes ....

....

Shalom, courage, and vision

Jesus said that the peace He gives us is unlike peace from any other source. How is it different?

His peace resides in our spirit and so can quieten a troubled mind and rampant emotions. This is not the absence of threat, stress, trouble, or loss but the active presence of a supernatural calmness of spirit freely given by God. It is robust, not fragile; it transcends human understanding and comes from the very presence of Father. Ensure the shalom of Jesus is a living and constant reality and not just a theological concept or belief. It's not enough to talk about it; we want to be manifesting it so all can see its effect on us!

This gift of peace is like being in the 'eye' of a storm that rages around us but doesn't harm us.

This incredible gift also allows vision to be birthed and carried in us and our courage to grow.

> 'Don't give up, don't be impatient; be entwined as one with the Lord and so be brave and courageous.' (Psalm 27:14)

> 'The peace which is me will be in you and will give you great confidence as you rest in Me.' (John 16:33)

Notes ....

....

....

....

'Guilt and shame' beliefs

There are multiple reasons why people get trapped in a cycle of ungodly beliefs about themselves. Guilt is a strategy of the enemy to immobilise us, and our upbringing, life experiences, and other people may all be utilised to compound and confirm these toxic lies.

An unhealthy obsession with our 'sinfulness', failings, and mistakes, or a perception that God is a stern father, will conspire to make it hard to break this downward spiral.

Many are hurt by being told that they are somehow inferior or less worthy, which clearly contradicts what God declares over us – that we are the apple of his eye!

Living with guilt or shame, for whatever reason, is both crippling and disempowering. It prevents us enjoying our true identity and fulfilling our God-given purpose. **We must be especially careful not to be a harsh judge of ourselves.**

> 'Everyone who believes is set free from sin and guilt – something the law had no power to do.' (Acts 13:39)

If you know you are frozen by guilt or shame and it stops you moving forward, I urge you to reach to God and experience His healing, freedom, and affirmation.

Notes ....

....

....

....

Affirmation and confidence

> 'Never let ugly or hateful words come from your mouth, but instead let your words become beautiful gifts that encourage others.' (Ephesians 4:29)

However, a prerequisite to doing this is to experience God's affirmation of us personally. Have you?

....

We can't love others if we don't love ourselves.

We can't bless others from a place of feeling useless or worthless. Holy Spirit stands poised to bring freedom from guilt and shame through Jesus and the affirmation of the Father. It's time to step away from our negative beliefs and cross over the threshold into another place where, by grace, we can live free, content, and fulfilled. (Notice I didn't include comfortable, predictable, easy, or hunky-dory!) From a place of knowing God affirms us, we discover an inner confidence in our spirit. Some mistake this for pride or individualism, but it's neither. It's a glorious, deep down, hard to shake sense of security because of our entwinedness with the Father, Jesus, and Holy Spirit. No longer needing to people please, perform, or be applauded by others. It's the best and most liberating thing I assure you.

Notes ....

....

....

Past regret and future anxiety

It's very apparent in the life and teaching of Jesus that it's good and healthy to 'live in the present' and all that it offers. Despite this advice, many have an unhealthy preoccupation with the past or the future and as a result often miss what is happening in the 'now'.

What percentage of your life is spent looking at either the past with its regrets, pain, and disappointments, or the future with its unknown and worrying possibilities? I have asked many this question, and the vast majority own up to 80% – which leaves only 20% for the present. How about you?

....

Looking back is not wrong, but having a focus there can be dispiriting, heavy, and painful. Similarly, looking forward isn't bad either, but a focus on it will often cause fear, anxiety, and preoccupation with 'what ifs'. Both these scenarios can be reduced to their proper place by allowing Jesus to be present in them, and by fixing most of our attention on the present moment, as Jesus invites us to do. What is in the foreground and what is the background of our thoughts will determine how well we manage to reside in the here and now. Put the present to the fore and the others towards the back.

Notes ....

....

....

....

Living in the now with joy

It's quite extraordinary how much joy and serenity is to be found in the practice of living life in the now.

It's hard to imagine until it's experienced!

Much needless anxiety is avoided, fears lose their grip, and stress is dramatically reduced.

Many of the 'what ifs' (future) that we fear never actually happen – so that's wasted imagination.

Many of the regrets and disappointments (past) can be healed and hope restored. Many things that God is saying and doing are missed because they are in the now and we are elsewhere (past or future). God is in the present, and that's where we find Him. When tomorrow comes, He will be there, but that will be the present. (Mull on this – it's profound once you get it!)

> 'Your Father cares deeply about even the smallest detail of your life, so don't worry'. (Matt 10:30)

> 'Don't let worry enter your life. Live above the anxious cares of your personal needs'. (Luke 12:29)

> 'Refuse to fear tomorrow but face each challenge one day at a time. Tomorrow will take care of itself.' (Matt 6:34)

Notes ....

....

....

....

Pretence

Pretence can be deliberate or unconscious – a ploy to deceive or simply a default state of mind, but either way it is the antithesis of all that God is. The Bible talks a lot about how much God dislikes hypocrisy, yet we tolerate it because it's so familiar and 'what everybody does'. Pretending is as damaging as lying is, to both ourselves and others. The only people Jesus condemned when on earth were the Pharisees, and it was for their two-faced, fake, and judgemental hypocrisy – their pretence to be super holy when they were far from that.

Being an authentic follower of Jesus leaves no room for us to pretend to be what we are not. It's what's in the heart that matters, not the external behaviour – especially when it's done to create a 'persona'.

Why is the desire to be thought well of by other people a bigger influence for us than that of honouring God?

....

Why do so many wear a 'mask' or project a false front, when God invites us to live honestly and authentically?

....

What starts out as a pretence to impress other people can so easily become comfortable and ends up with us believing it ourselves. Consider if this might be true of you.

Notes ....

....

Integrity

Over the last 50 years, my personal experience has been that many people have a distinct absence of integrity – especially when under pressure. Sadly, this has been particularly prevalent amongst Christians – the very people called to live, breathe, and display integrity!

In order to be someone of integrity, we must lose the desire and practice to pretend.

Be careful what you say, but let your 'yes' be yes and your 'No' be no.

It is such a precious thing to have relationships that are based on and shaped by loving integrity – I highly value them and protect that integrity.

The current generation is much less tolerant of unreality and sees though pretence quickly – they are looking for a new depth of authenticity. Will you help them?

> 'Discard every form of dishonesty and lying so that you will be known as one who always speaks the truth'. (Eph 4:25)

> 'Set yourself apart as a model of a life lived with dignity and integrity.' (Titus 2:7)

> 'Abandon every form of evil, deceit, hypocrisy, jealousy, and slander.' (1 Peter 2:1)

Notes ....

....

....

Disunity and division

It's undeniable that the church has an appalling track record when it comes to unity. What makes this both ironic and catastrophic is that our love for each other is the key message Jesus asks us to demonstrate to the world at large. I can't see how we could have got that more wrong. Many Christians accept that the plethora of denominations, streams, and groups are not God's intention for His Church but continue to perpetuate them. I believe God's calling time on this situation! Division in the family of God is an affront; it's dishonouring, destructive, disabling, disreputable, and a disgrace.

The burning question here is not how the church can fix itself but how we as individuals can be those who display unity rather than division.

Ask Holy Spirit what needs to change in you.

....

Judgemental criticism by one believer towards another is unacceptable yet widely seen and practised. Having different interpretations of scripture, different doctrinal imperatives, or conflicting convictions are absolutely no justification for allowing or contributing to disunity. If there's not unity, there's disunity – no middle ground.

Notes ....

....

....

....

Oneness of kindred spirits

This is a time when God is calling us back to basics and to relegate all that divides us. This is virtually impossible within an existing church structure, and that presents a massive obstacle to many. The Bible is crystal clear that it is God who creates unity between those who have a relationship with Him. We do not and cannot create that unity (despite the ecumenical attempts to do so). However, we can break or destroy it. It's something God brings when we flow together with Him, not a human organisational outcome. The historical rationale for attempting unity has been theological agreement – but no more! Dynamic, tender, honouring, peer-level oneness can be enjoyed safely, happily, and powerfully when there is oneness of 'spirit'.

'Like-minded' is superseded by 'kindred spirit'.

This unity occurs when Holy Spirit calls the shots and people flow with Him. I see this in action so know it's not a pipe dream. Are you willing to lay down your personal preferences, prejudices, and doctrinal opinions in order to discover the reality of this kind of oneness?

The joy and laughter that is found when we are united with others is indescribable and 'a pearl of great price'. Of course, it's wonderful, as it was His plan all along!

Notes ....

....

....

....

Management leadership

During my life and career, I've had hundreds of interactions with church leadership teams, ministers, charismatic leaders, and organisational heads, and my overriding experience is that most churches are run like businesses with managers in charge. Organisational structure (usually hierarchical) is the most widely used model employed by leaders, who generally function like CEOs or MDs. Whilst this is a viable and effective form of leadership model and style in many arenas, it's mostly a disaster for oversight of a spiritual family.

It leads, sometimes unintentionally, to control, the manipulation and suppression of individuals, inequality, racism, misogyny, and even abuse. The collateral damage and fallout from this church model has been devastating and far reaching, not least over the last 50 years. Additionally, the activity of Holy Spirit and the headship of Jesus are undermined and frustrated by human insecurity and the need to be in charge. This is changing (at God's instigation) – leaders, don't get caught out by the shift! If you don't lead, rather than blaming those who've been or are leaders, consider how you might need a changed heart and attitude towards those you influence.

Notes ....

....

....

....

....

Family dynamics

There are many ways of characterising what godly leadership is, but it should never include control or manipulation of others. Leaders who function as a 'healthy' mum and/or dad to a family is, perhaps, the easiest model to explore. The heart of a godly, kind, gentle, and loving parent is vastly differently from the motivation and approach of a manager. This contrast of leadership has never been more visible in the church than now, but the management style has a limited shelf life, I believe. Thankfully, there's been much teaching and ministry on the Father heart of God, but what is needed now is people who have that same heart and care for others from that perspective. We don't need more leaders in the family, we need more mums and dads. My adult children are not under my jurisdiction, but our 'peer' relationship means that we dialogue from a place of love and honour for each other. I don't wield authority or demand allegiance, compliance, or obedience, or dictate what happens in their lives. Amazingly, this works if you have the right heart before God, in His family too. I know from personal experience. Ask Holy Spirit what internal adjustments He'd like you to make.

Notes ....

....

....

....

....

....

Platform centred

Living in a world of celebrity culture and having a church history that is patriarchal have both contributed to a church model that is 'front led'. The preacher has a pulpit, the worship band has a platform, guests have reserved seats, and leaders have a high profile. Whenever there's a meeting, everything is platform-centric. We look to those who have a title, position, experience, or reputation to lead and direct us, to spoon-feed us, and to keep things under control. This model replicates the lecture, the gig, the personality, the management style, and performance mentality that can be found outside the church; however, its use within God's family is being dismantled – please take note if you are a platform person!

Any structure that facilitates this front-led obsession needs to be filed away and replaced by a better way. Reserve the platform for exceptional times, let spiritual life and unity flourish away from the platform.

No more performances, celebrities, services, 'eyes front', or control please – it's fraught with danger (as we've seen) and mitigates against Holy Spirit and the pre-eminence of Jesus.

Notes ....

....

....

....

....

....

....

Table focused

I've personally heard the Lord say, 'Be curators of the table rather than people of the platform.'

Maybe pause and think about that for a while.

....

Rather than investing huge amounts of time and money into programmes, rotas, and public meetings, let our focus be on Jesus and His presence being 'known' in our homes around our tables. Nice idea, but easier said than done I hear you say. I know, but it illustrates the magnitude of the seismic shift we are in the middle of at this time. Conversations that include God are better than sermons, ordinary speech is better than religious jargon, felt reality is more impactful than a lecture, and encounter is preferable to information. Letting people meet Jesus in their everyday life is more impactful than attending church. The only requirement for this to be amazing is that Jesus be real and present in your heart and life for others to see. Be normal, be real, display Jesus, and then let those around your 'table' see that.

If your Jesus vibe is dim, let Him make it brighter – just ask and give Him unconditional permission.

Amazing things occur around tables and food!

Notes ....

....

....

....

Institution, rule-keeping, and religious rigidity

I think most people, except maybe religious zealots, would be averse to the rigid adherence to religious rules. We've all read about the Pharisees and their harsh intolerance, never mind Jesus' criticism of them for their oppression of those who 'break the rules'. However, centuries of church history reveal the tendency towards exactly this rule of law as exemplified by the religious leaders of Jesus' day. It can still be seen in every stream of the Christian church in the 21st century. The reason this matters so much is that it's the opposite of God's desire for us to know freedom, love, peace, joy, forgiveness, honour, and unity. We do not live under the law of the old covenant but in the new covenant implemented by Jesus.

God is looking at our heart not our orthodoxy. Once again, the most pertinent question is how is this relevant to you.

Are you oppressed by others in this way?

Do you demand this of others?

Do you inflict this on yourself (even unintentionally)?

Ask Holy Spirit to show you (journal below).

Notes ....

....

....

....

....

....

Spontaneity, exploration, and wonder

Thinking that 'safety' and 'order' come from rule-keeping and control is to misunderstand the freedom that Jesus offers to His followers. There is wonderful joy, release, acceptance, and freedom in wide-eyed wonder, child-like exploration, and creative spontaneity – truly there is. God rarely does anything the same way twice, yet we want to get into repetitive, boring, and predictable patterns so we know where we stand! If the person you were created to be is held captive, restricted, or boxed in, I urge you to break out of your prison/box and fly free with Holy Spirit. You do not require permission. When we are no longer limited by the parameters of our finite mind, our spirit is free to explore and discover like never before. Exploration of heaven's secrets and mysteries needs an intellect that is aware of its inadequacy to comprehend them. Soaring in our spirit will take us to places and bring revelation that our cognitive capability never will.

What restrictions are 'in place' that impact or limit you being able to be creative, spontaneous, or adventurous? It's a personal choice to leave the box and swim in the bottomless ocean of God's love and playfulness.

Notes ....

....

....

....

....

Power-seeking, status, and position

It's a sad fact that both history and the current day clearly demonstrate the appeal to many of status, reputation, fame, and position. The drivenness of wanting control, the opportunity to dominate others, and the lust for power and pride all make this temptation hard to resist for some. Tragically, this is as prevalent within Christendom as anywhere else. How that must delight the enemy and grieve God. It's not part of kingdom life, it's not Jesus' example, and it flies in the face of His teaching about the first being last and the last first. Yet I have encountered this 'lording it' over others in church leadership more times and in multiple places than I can count. Hierarchy must be utterly deconstructed. Leadership is not a career option or gained by dint of strong character or loudest voice. This cannot be a hallmark of the family of God any longer.

Are there people that you have unhealthy control over?

Are there people who've ungodly control over you?

Have you crucified the desire for position and any lust for power?

Do you influence others without ulterior motive?

Notes ....

....

....

....

....

....

....

....

Purity, maturity, and humility

The one place above all others where 'power-crazed' people should not be is in the church. Living life inextricably entwined with God results in an increase in maturity, humility, and purity (the total antithesis of the previous page). Jesus exuded authority without having position, or status. He exercised quiet power and wisdom without hype, and He felt no need to justify or defend himself. These traits were the result of His close communion with his Father. We can live in this way too. If we stop striving to be 'better' and go deeper in our relationship with God, these things will start to grow and become visible in our lives.

The mistake I made was to try harder, when the key was to let God bring about the 'maturing' via a closer relationship. Dying to self leads to fulfilment, being a lover of God births purity without effort or obligation, and enjoying affirmation from God is liberating and blissful. Striving, stressing, people pleasing, and the need to seek reputation and earn God's favour melt away. Contentment comes as we mature in spirit.

The less we interfere or strive, the more He does!

Notes ....

....

....

....

....

....

....

Pleading prayer

One of the occurances in this current reset is a recalibration and redefinition of intercession. Often when we take our 'shopping lists' to God we assume that He is there to solve our problems, resolve issues, and fix our stuff. Whilst it's true that He cares for us with a tender heart, He is so much more than an 'agony aunt', or a hard to please master, or even an extra emergency service! We do not need to beg God to do something – that misunderstands the relationship between Him and us. When we are asking God for some intervention or solution, let's **first** ask Him if He has something to show us or say to us. Often, in my experience, He either has a more important topic that He wants us to focus on, or sometimes He is wanting us to be the intervention and the solution ourselves. More often than you think, He says, 'Why are you asking me when I have empowered you to make a difference?' There isn't a loss of respect or reverence, but there is the revelation that, as mature children of God, we have been given His authority to speak into and over people and situations, both local and global. Long or repetitive requests in prayer need to be substituted by powerful declarations imbued with power, humility, love, and confidence.

Notes ....

....

....

....

....

....

Declaration

There is a dynamic impact of declaration that is:

- ➢ partnering with God's heart and will
- ➢ shot through with compassion and love
- ➢ from a place of intimacy with God
- ➢ wise and kind
- ➢ confident in who God says we are
- ➢ rooted in faith
- ➢ carrying Holy Spirit wisdom
- ➢ devoid of self-promotion or reputation

This revelation and practice will transform and redeem what it addresses.

Do you need to recalibrate how you pray?

....

There are traps to avoid of course, like arrogance, pride, affirmation of others, superiority, self-confidence, and method. However, the wonder of walking in the fullness of what Jesus calls us to be and do far outweighs being disciplined and staying on the straight and narrow.

Rest and trust in the Three and see what happens. Spend more time with God on your own and less on religious activity.

Notes ....

....

Bible 'worship'

Anything or anyone who is more important (or equally important) to us than Jesus is highly likely to be an issue and is probably idolatrous. The challenge is that this applies to 'good' things and people not just the other kind! I write this with some trepidation, and after a journey of years with Holy Spirit, but this wrong focus can, and often does, apply to our view of the Bible.

It is common with Christians/churches to place the written word on an equal or greater footing than the person who is the living word – Jesus.

Check your response to this statement: what thoughts or feelings are triggered in you and why?

....

....

Part of the reason for this inverted priority is that we tend to substitute the more easily understood book for the more challenging and costly reality of a relationship with its author.

Why do we want to just trust the map book when we have a resident Guide?

The latter is more trustworthy and reliable than the former if you have authentic connection with Him.

Notes ....

....

....

Holy Spirit reliance

Few would dispute that Holy Spirit is vital to our spiritual wellbeing and growth. Religion can manage without His presence, but followers of Jesus cannot. Jesus even said that it was better for us disciples that He returned to heaven so that Holy Spirit could be released to the earth to reside with and in us.

If we are enjoying ongoing authentic 'communion' with Him, we are in a much 'safer' place than if we have to rely on particular doctrines, scriptural interpretations, or opinions. This is a challenge for most of us as it involves 'unlearning the engrained'.

This does not mean we disregard the Bible, just that we relegate it to its proper place of subjection to Holy Spirit revelation; both are important but not equally.

God yearns for connection with us that is relational, emotional, and vibrant rather than simply conceptual, intellectual, and dry. Be honest with Him and yourself as to which kind of connection you currently have.

....

This total reliance on Holy Spirit brings us to a new reality where we have much more peace, comfort, calm, confidence, hope, joy, stability, self-control, maturity, and fulfilment. It's amazing!

Notes ....

....

....

....

Jargon

This is something that many agree is not helpful, and yet the vast majority of Christians still employ words that are never used in everyday language and that are mind bogglingly baffling to those who are not 'in the know'. This very easily leads to a language that is religious, intimidating, and unclear. Doctrinal terms and phrases, archaic words, and 'church' speak are often what we hide behind. We do this without thinking, even subconsciously, because it is engrained in us and what we have been taught is the acceptable norm. Jesus was careful to use conversation that related to the everyday life of His hearers (much to the annoyance of the religious-leaders). The parables He used were 'normal' – life-oriented, not religious focused; it was the language of the masses, not of the privileged few.

Theological terminology really is unnecessary outside of academic debate – let's explain doctrine without jargon but rather with ordinary everyday words. You'll be staggered by how much more meaningful it becomes, even to you! Using archaic language misleads people to think our faith has little relevance in a 21st-century world. Why not try a 10-day 'jargon' fast (including prayers). It's harder than you would expect!

Notes ....

....

....

....

....

Plain speaking

When we drop 'christianese' from our vocabulary and employ normal words, there is a greater relevance, authenticity, clarity, and impact to the message we carry and the mission we have been given. Let's talk about Jesus in words everyone can understand, not about doctrine that few can grasp. Introduce the person of Jesus rather than just teaching about Him.

Plain speaking also involves us being honest, clear, and transparent (from a kind, gentle, and loving heart).

No hypocrisy, duplicity, lying, cruelty, slander, flattery, disparagement, or manipulation with words.

It's time to master the tongue and be uber careful what we say.

Let our 'yes' mean yes and our 'no' mean no.

Let our words encourage, honour, inspire, and love God, others, and ourselves.

Let's not mask any of our own unreality by hiding behind terminology we often don't fully understand ourselves. Let what we say express the reality of our internal relationship with the divine, and if it doesn't then let's not say it!

Control of our tongue is a mark of spiritual maturity.

Notes ....

....

....

....

....

....

The numbers game

This topic focuses in particular on our concept of church but has application to many other things too. Society has largely accepted the idea that big is always better, that globalisation is great, and that it's ok to obscure the uniqueness of the individual for the sake of the whole. Sadly, this opinion can also be widely found inside church (as we know it). Individuals are asked to 'sign up' to someone else's vision and mission rather than explore their own. It's said that the bigger the local church is numerically, the bigger impact it can have on its locality. Evangelism can be thinly disguised recruitment, controlling leadership is necessary for 'unity', and multiple programmes are required for expansion and development.

Growth as a goal is fine if there is a parallel emphasis on health. The healthy maturation of either a church group or an individual is of greater significance than numbers. It's time to switch the focus on numerical growth to spiritual growth (they are not the same thing at all).

We need to collaborate with Holy Spirit and recalibrate in order to displace this obsession with numerical expansion with a new priority of spiritual health and maturity.

Notes ....

....

....

....

....

Health before growth

As followers of Jesus, our desire is surely to become more and more like Him, to think, speak, and behave as He did. This is a journey of increasing spiritual health and maturing which is measurable, visible, ongoing, and transformative.

The impact and influence on our world is rooted in a person's character and in their 'Christlikeness', not in strategy, personality, or programmes.

Group unity emerges when individuals are spiritually healthy, not when there are partisan factions, a lowest common denominator, or an imposed agenda/vision. Worship is on another level when our healthy focus is on God rather than on our own needs.

Leadership is so positive when that person is spiritually healthy rather than needy, insecure, and professional. None of this is new thought, but it may be a new reality. **It's much less about what we know and much more about who we know. How 'healthy' is your spirit?**

....

Spiritual health is the fruit of an ever-deepening relationship with God, not formed from knowledge, study, and theological prowess. It's simple not hard work when it's personal, relational, and experiential.

Notes ....

....

....

Acquaintance

Throughout this book, I've repeatedly mentioned the difference between intellectual and spiritual reality, between concept and experience, between theory and actuality, and between religious and authentic. It is easy to think that head knowledge and heart knowledge are the same thing when they are not. We can be deluded that we enjoy the latter when what we have is the former. This is a centuries-old con by Satan to rob the children of God of their identity, to create the illusion of relationship, and to nullify the power of God that resides in each of us. Acquaintance isn't enough!

Being acquainted with someone is very different from knowing them, and knowing them is not the same as being in a personal relationship with them.

It is vital that we know the difference and that we identify the nature of our connection with God.

Do you talk at God or with God?

Do you ask God for things more than you listen to Him?

Do you know Him merely in your head or your spirit?

Do you know about Him, or do you experience Him?

Does it matter if your theology isn't your experience?

Are you comfortable to chill in His tangible presence?

How intimate does your relationship with God feel?

Notes ....

....

....

Entwinement/Intimacy

The ultimate human relationship is one that includes intimacy and fusion, with each party 'losing' themselves in the other. This exclusivity and vulnerability, when contributed by both partners, results in a loving, secure, beautiful, and exciting journey of discovery.

What many don't know is that this is the model for our relationship with God. It is not only possible (I can vouch for that), but the great desire for His heart all along.

This incredible and real closeness brings mind-blowing encounters with Him that turn doctrine into reality (it often redefines or reinterprets it too).

After a period of time enjoying this intimacy, we find ourselves increasingly and inextricably entwined with the Three (like strands of a rope); Their perspectives, characteristics, and opinions start to rub off on us. We find insight, wisdom, love, compassion, patience, and joy increase in us without any effort on our part. **It's sanctification by osmosis!** (Sorry about the 'jargon'.)

This is revelatory and can't be taught.

This is life changing not a one off.

This is personal and can't be adopted second hand.

This is relational not a method.

Entwinement with the Trinity is the achievable goal!

Notes ....

....

....

....

Recalibration is required

A God-decreed paradigm shift is not only underway but is being accelerated by Him.

This shift is not a 'tweak' or an 'adjustment'; it's a seismic change from being 'head led' to 'heart led'.

This is true for every aspect and element of creation. It's a total recalibration that leaves virtually nothing in sync (until it has been recalibrated).

Much of what people 'know' is being flipped on its head. This is as true in the body of Christ as outside of it.

Virtually nothing will be left untouched or unchanged.

What we are entering will probably feel alien and uncomfortable, but this is good as it motivates us to maintain permanent dependence on, and reference to Holy Spirit. A shift of power is underway from formal, Institutional, managerial hierarchy to informal, opt-in decision making that is peer driven.

Power is moving from the few to the many.

There is a change from leader-driven to participatory group wisdom. From hoarding and controlling power to empowerment and release.

In commerce we prioritise people before profit. (God's favour follows our obedience, so profit is a consequence not a goal.)

There's a changed mindset that puts contribution above acquisition. (What can I bring and give rather than what do I get out of this.)

Our impact is vastly more important than our income.

Integrity, humility, and generosity are foundational.

Recalibration leads us:

To demonstrate the heart of Father (and so glorify Him). To live from a place of constant communion with God.

To be fruitful and fulfilled.

To bless and empower others and curate creation.

To contribute to the wellbeing of all.

To express the creativity implanted by God.

To 'live out' the command to love our neighbour.

To discover, invent, develop, and release the 'new' that sits in heaven.

To bring godly influence to the marketplace and release blessing to others.

To empower others to be fully themselves and to follow their dreams/destiny.

To express collaboration and unity rather than competition (as exemplified in the Trinity).

To develop in spiritual maturity and character.

Can you let Holy Spirit deconstruct your theology?

....

Are you open to be 'recalibrated' by God?

....

Will you invest more of yourself in finding intimacy?

....

There is always more to be discovered!

Part 2

CLARITY

Clearing the fog and decluttering from the conventional to facilitate revelation and momentum.

He who dwells (abides) in the shelter of the Most High will remain secure and at rest in the shadow of the Almighty (whose power no enemy can withstand).

I say of the Lord, 'He is my refuge and fortress, my God in whom I trust, with great confidence, and on whom I rely.'

Psalm 91:1–2

Contents

**When God asks a question,
He's not launching an interrogation
but inviting us on a journey
of redemption and restoration.**

Introduction

Much of Christendom is engaged in replicating the story of the Emperor's clothes, but God is calling for a reset that reflects His reality rather than a religious illusion.

There is a fine line between genius and madness. The same can be said for most of the topics covered in the following chapters. So often the defining factor is heart motive.

It is vital to be truthful and honest with ourselves and acknowledge our 'dominant' reality. If we are shaped by our physical reality rather than our spiritual reality, our faith will be more conceptual than experiential. How self-aware are we of our connection with the Divine?

Things may be very similar in their outward appearance but radically different on the inside. The Pharisees were accused of that by Jesus; whitewashed tombs that belie the death inside them.

Jesus was the ultimate modeller of 'reading the heart' rather than just listening to words being spoken. It's advisable to have the spiritual wisdom and discernment to know 'what is what' and 'which is which' in this time of great transition. Safe navigation requires maturity of character, a wise and tender heart, and clarity of vision.

The simple chapters are designed to provoke thought, prayer, and discussion with Holy Spirit, and with each other. The material isn't written sequentially, so you can dip in and out or read the page that catches your eye.

My hope and prayer is that you will find a deeper relationship with God and greater spiritual clarity whilst pondering what you read and hear in your spirit.

Jonathan

1 Distinguish between the counterfeit and the genuine

Counterfeit: The whole point of anything counterfeit is to fool you into thinking you are enjoying the genuine article when, in fact, you are not. Being able to distinguish the real from the fake requires intimate knowledge of the authentic original. To assume that you will recognise the counterfeit is both dangerous and arrogant unless you have the ability to discern the difference. It's a costly error to mistake the false for the true. You might be led to believe that a person possesses something which they don't, that they have a nest egg where one doesn't exist or a resource that they can't actually deliver when the proverbial hits the fan. To only make this discovery in the white heat of trial, loss, or suffering is devastating and causes both disillusionment and disappointment.

Genuine: There is joy, fulfilment, and deep contentment when someone knows for sure that what they have is the genuine article – the real deal. It becomes a well to draw from, a resource to benefit from, and an investment that yields a great reward. There is assurance, expectation, and hope that all will be well both in the present and the future. Be wowed by God!

Consider:

How do we know we have not been hoodwinked?

What strategies might our enemy adopt to con us?

Do you communicate with God for yourself or for others?

Dare you ask Holy Spirit to reveal what's real or fake in you?

2 Distinguish between weakness and meekness

Weakness: This is not limited to the physical but extends to the mental, emotional, and spiritual. Dictionary definitions include words like feeble, unsound, indecisive, intimidated, timid, exhausted, and sickly. Scripture talks about not having a spirit of timidity but rather a 'sound' mind, about not being double-minded or faint-hearted, and about strengthening our tired hands and weak knees – all expressions of weakness. Followers of Jesus are called to care for the weak, to champion those marginalised and ignored by society, and so are to be those who are not weak themselves. This is not a chance to be domineering or overbearing but to be stable and strong in God, to exude love, and to be secure in our relationship with Him.

Meekness: Many misinterpret meekness as weakness because they can look similar (hence the need to distinguish between them). Meekness is 'strength under the control of love', meaning the difference is the heart motivation not the external expression. Meekness evidences itself when a person is gentle, generously loving, tenderly humble, patient, peaceable, modest, and unpretentious yet confident, secure, courageous, wise, discerning, and affirmed by their connection with Father, Jesus, and Holy Spirit. This is a position of great strength, peace, assurance, stability, security, purity, and fulfilment. There is no longer any need to perform for plaudits, to people please, or to grow a profile.

Consider:

Ask yourself where you are on the weak to meek spectrum.

Now ask Holy Spirit the same question about yourself.

3 Distinguish between concept and reality

Concept: Knowing something intellectually is not the same as experiencing the reality of it, however convinced we are of its validity. The concept that God loves us is utterly different from regularly experiencing His love. The first is information, and the second is reality. The former is absolute truth, but the latter is our personal truth. Sadly, there are many who mistake their knowledge for a relationship and so never push on to discover the personal reality of what they believe. This accounts for much of the 'gap' between what the Bible describes and the everyday reality of our lives. It's of such foundational importance to understand the nature of our connection with God. Is it based on what we believe or on who know?

Reality: It's hard to imagine what experiential reality is like from a place of theoretical existence. However, once we make the transition, everything changes – everything! Concepts that required effort to live out become second nature, ideas that puzzled us are no longer a concern, and our relationship with God becomes tangible, vibrant, and intimate. The contrast is shocking but exhilarating.

Truth is ignited by experience – what a joy, and what a relief!

Consider:

Honestly and objectively ask yourself how much of your spiritual life is based on beliefs, and how much as a result of your interaction with the person of Jesus?

Is God real to you predominately in your head or your heart?

4 Distinguish between information and revelation

Information: Information is the acquisition of knowledge, the collection of data, the garnering of facts and opinions that cause us to form the beliefs and opinions that we hold to (our world view). There is nothing wrong in this – in fact it's both healthy and helpful, but there is need for complete clarity in discerning the difference between this and 'revelation'. Information is primarily gathered and filtered through our mind, whereas revelation is received and birthed in our spirit.

Revelation: Revelation is something that Holy Spirit tells/shows/communicates to us personally. It is the desire of God for every one of his children that we engage in a two-way relationship and communication and that includes you!

When another person has a revelation from God which they share, it's vital that we realise this is a second-hand revelation if we 'adopt' it as our own. Before 'owning' it as ours, we take it to God for application, interpretation, or clarification. What He reveals then transitions that revelation into first hand rather than second. Be careful not to confuse revelation and an opinion (yours or somebody else's).

Consider:

Are there words, opinions, or prophecies which you have 'adopted' that have negatively impacted your life and adversely affected your relationship with God?

Do you accept that God wants two-way communication with you as much as he does with anyone else?

5 Distinguish between religious adherence and discipleship

Religious adherence: The Biblical example we have of this is the religious leaders of Jesus' day. They were preoccupied with applying God's law and will (as they saw it) to the letter and to the exclusion of all else. They were so busy fulfilling their role of 'representing God's truth', so busy judging and 'correcting' all who they disagreed with, that they failed to communicate the heart of God and completely missed the arrival of God's Messiah. Oops!

There is no shortage, in the 21st century, of people with the same mindset of believing they have a duty to 'defend truth' and correct those who disagree with them yet fail to perceive what God is doing at this time. The loyalty and faithfulness of those who follow Jesus are to a person rather than a religion-, a creed-, or a man-instituted label. There is a clear divergence already underway that sees a widening chasm between devotees of the Christian religion and followers of Jesus. These may sound similar, but in practice they are different.

Discipleship: A radical departure from the old and historic understanding of God was what the disciples gained from Jesus and the Pharisees never grasped. The same is true today. Discipleship is characterised by love not duty and obligation, by unity not division, by compassion not judgement, by demonstrating the heart of Jesus not defending our theology, by drawing people not driving them, and by freedom not regulations.

Consider:

What or who are you loyal to? A person, a creed, or a label? Is your relationship with God one of love of obligation?

6 Distinguish between inertia and rest

Inertia: This is associated with apathy, laziness, stupor, and a lack of progress. It's a negative without reward, it's usually counterproductive to the 'kingdom coming', and it's not honouring to God. However, external inactivity can be misinterpreted as inertia when in fact it is rest.

Rest: There is a lot of focus and talk about 'entering God's rest' and the enormous benefits it offers, but those of us who are doers find this hard to develop as a practice, and those of us who don't understand this misinterpret rest as inertia – doing nothing. There's a need to clarify. Rest is to sit to 'wait on God', and it's where we actively engage our spirits in stillness. **Revelation rarely comes to the busy**.

Inertia is passive, but rest in God is active, even when there is no physical or mental exertion or activity. There is so much to uniquely learn and discover in the place of waiting. Embrace any opportunity to 'come aside' (as Jesus did), to be still and commune with Father. So many are too busy to find the time to do this yet it's a key to deepening our spiritual life.

It's vital to know when our inactivity is inertia and when it is rest/waiting. Let's be 'doing' from a place of 'being' and not even attempting vice versa.

Consider:

Do you know the difference between inertia and rest; have you experienced either?

Do you know how to 'do' from a place of 'be'?

Does waiting for God irritate and frustrate you?

If you don't have 'rest' as part of your life, what can change?

7 Distinguish between reputation and significance

Reputation: The world we live in is so limited in its way of valuing people that from an early age most of us strive to acquire a reputation of some kind in order to feel significant. There is a desire/need to be regularly affirmed by others as to our value and contribution in their world. Whilst some of these things have some merit, it can mask our needy lack of self-worth, our drive for acceptance, and our emotional insecurity.

Don't fall for the lie that no reputation means you are not important or significant to God, or that you cannot influence the world around you.

Significance: There are many ways in which people determine who is significant and, therefore, who is not.

We look at a person's qualifications, career, experience, talent, and giftings, and their influence, following, and reputation. Jesus presents a very different value mindset for evaluating our personal significance – e.g., the first shall be last and the last first. Many of the most 'significant' in the kingdom of God are hidden, ignored, persecuted, or at least unnoticed. As followers of Jesus, we need to be alert as to how we determine who and what is significant. The values of heaven rather than of earth are needed to accurately perceive what is 'significant' to God. You'll be surprised!

Consider:

Are you feeling insignificant? Why is that?

Who's important among believers; why do you think that?

What does Holy Spirit show you about your own significance?

Are you comparing yourself to others and their reputation?

8 Distinguish between familiarity and intimacy

Familiarity: We can be familiar with something or someone, know a lot about them, engage with them on a regular basis, and enjoy the connection we have. Or I can describe somebody I know in great detail so that you become familiar with that person, but that is taken to another level when you actually meet that person face to face and have your own conversation. Familiarity, relationally speaking, is better than being unfamiliar or ignorant, or a stranger, but it's not the ultimate possibility. Interaction that is intimate is way beyond familiarity or knowledge.

Intimacy: Most Christians would agree that God is not a remote, far-off figure, since Jesus created a way for us to be reunited with Him. Some realise that He is not a stern, harsh master waiting to punish us, but only a few seem to experience a relationship with God that can be described as 'intimate'. The Bible describes us as the bride and Jesus the Bridegroom. This is not a gift to be fearful of but rather to revel in. Where familiarity may breed contempt, intimacy does the reverse, and I assure that there is no loss of reverence or respect, only a deepening love and joyful, uncoerced dependence. This is an extraordinary gift that is offered to all followers of Jesus.

Consider:

Does the thought of intimacy with God scare or offend you?

How much of your relationship with God is based in 'familiarity', and how much as an outcome of 'intimacy'?

Why not take some time to let Holy Spirit bring revelation?

9 Distinguish between knowledge and wisdom

Knowledge: The pursuit and acquisition of knowledge and information is worthwhile, profitable, and to be encouraged. However, your spirit can take you places beyond any intellectual capability or cognitive capacity, and so knowledge has limits to what it can deliver.

Venerating knowledge can limit our exploration of the spiritual and delude us into thinking we perceive something when we don't. Note that having knowledge is good but not a mark of maturity. Head knowledge has limitations, but knowing in our 'knower' is different. As we develop our cardio gnosis (heart knowledge), we discover that the impact of applying what we know requires a spiritual gift, wisdom.

Wisdom: Although some wisdom usually comes with age and life experience, there is also the gift from God of spiritual wisdom. This is a different lens; it flourishes in our spirit and leads to very different conclusions and actions than when we rely on natural human wisdom. This wisdom helps us to handle the words, gifts, words of knowledge, and prophecies we receive from God with compassion, love, humility, and grace. That is when spiritual maturity becomes evident. Rely on the wisdom of God rather than the 'things you know' – it's a very different journey believe me.

Consider:

How much of what you know of God is in your head?

Is there discrepancy between this and what your spirit senses?

How do you tell the difference?

Is any 'ministry' you exercise marinated in wisdom?

10 Distinguish between submission and surrender

Submission: This generally means the subduing of someone by another with greater power or strength. Militarily, it's the vanquishing of an army or nation by another stronger one. Spiritually speaking, we talk about submitting to God's will and demands and subjugating our preferences and desires. This implies (even if it's subconscious) that God demands our surrender and that we are to do as we are told and so avoid His displeasure. This can lead to us giving in reluctantly, even grudgingly and feeling resentful of a demanding Father.

Of course, we want to honour God but not from a position of obligation, duty, or imposition.

Surrender: Often this word is synonymous with submission, but I want to paint a very different picture. Rather than this being the overpowering of the 'weaker' to the stronger, let's consider the imagery of 'surrendering' yourself into the arms of the one who loves you – willingly, joyfully, eagerly, gladly, and passionately abandoning yourself with total trust, security, and anticipation into the embrace of your lover.

This is an incredibly different scenario, with far-reaching implications, consequences, and transformation.

It's impossible to describe in words this experience of full and glad surrender to Father, Jesus, and Holy Spirit, but once that intimacy is discovered nothing less will satisfy.

Consider:

Do you surrender to God as a master or a lover?

Do you enjoy that surrender, or is it given out of obligation?

Are you aware that God longs for your love so much more than your obedience?

11 Distinguish between behavioural change and transformation

Behavioural change: The challenge here is that if you look only at externals change of behaviour and transformation can look identical. It's not hard (at least in the short term) to change our words and actions so they masquerade as an internal and permanent change. This fools many people much of the time, but not God, and not mature, discerning people responding to the impulses and revelation of Holy Spirit. Living like this is exhausting and dispiriting, and keeping up the pretence will likely bring burnout or disillusionment. Its cause may be to maintain our reputation, to receive the approval of others, or even to avoid the truth.

How different things would be if people no longer felt the need to pretend or wear a mask.

Transformation: Transformational change is always internal first and then external differences are the fruit of that. Transformation is authentic, permanent, and sometimes costly. It will affect your attitudes, demeanour, emotions, thoughts, and subsequently your words and actions.

God's heart is to redeem every part of us to become more like Jesus, and Holy Spirit is tasked with bringing about that glorious, redemptive transformation, although it does require our permission and collaboration!

Consider:

Have you created a mask that hides your internal reality?

What might be the reason you choose to do this?

Do you realise how toxic the effects of self-comparison are?

Ask Holy Spirit to show what's real and what's not, in you.

12 Distinguish between opportunity and destiny

Opportunity: Having the chance to 'take' an opportunity, whether big or small, is a regular occurrence in life. Often it may open a door, progress a career, or change circumstances for us, so it can rightly be viewed as a good thing to accept. However, seizing an opportunity can also result in us being too busy, and therefore overburdened, exhausted, and not able to see the wood for the trees. If we say 'yes' too often, it can become detrimental for our health and wellbeing, but worse still it may mean we say no to things that are more important and of greater significance for us. The wisdom to know when to say yes and when to say no is vital. It's not just shunning poor options but also declining 'good' ones.

Destiny: One way we can be wise in our choice to run with or pass up an opportunity is to ask the question, 'is this option part of my destiny?' As our Creator gave each of us a unique identity and destiny, it makes sense to a) discover what they both are, and b) align ourselves and our choices with them as closely as possible. This saves us a lot of hassle and getting ourselves into 'dead-end' situations; it helps us make informed and godly choices and brings fulfilment and peace. Being able to distinguish between these two things is an expression of godly wisdom.

Consider:

Can you discern between opportunity and destiny?

Do you know who God created you to 'be' and your purpose?

God tells us to ask Him for wisdom – do you often do that?

Ask Holy Spirit to shed more light on this for you personally.

13 Distinguish between selfishness and self-care

Selfishness: I don't think it's necessary to spend much time explaining this; most people understand it and dislike it in others. However, we need to monitor it in ourselves as well, knocking it on the head any time it manifests. It's clearly labelled in the Bible as being ungodly and to be avoided.

We are called to put caring for others as a higher priority than our desires, demands, preferences, and needs.

> 'Abandon every expression of selfishness. Possess a greater concern for what matters to others instead of your own interests.'
>
> (Phil 2: 4)

Self-care: The opposite of being selfish is to be selfless, and that's a good thing. However, this has led to many not understanding that self-care is something very different from selflessness, and we need to discern the difference.

It matters that we look after our physical, mental, emotional, and spiritual health. This way we honour our Creator, we are a better version of ourselves, and we have the love, patience, and wisdom to care for others. Flirting with fatigue, risking burnout, and being too busy to listen all dilute or remove our ability to meaningfully bless those around us. Thus, unselfish self-care is a wise practice that has many benefits.

Eliminate hurry, sit with Jesus, meditate on what Holy Spirit shows you. Decline to facilitate stress or take thoughts 'captive', and watch less TV, be outdoors more, listen more than you talk, count to ten more often, and learn to breathe properly.

Consider:

Do you think you are selfish or selfless?

Do you engage in regular self-care? Is your life too hurried?

14 Distinguish between self-fulfilment and ministry

Self-fulfilment: I have interacted with many who exercise a 'ministry', and something I've repeatedly observed and discovered is that many gain their sense of self-worth and fulfilment primarily from ministering. Many times the need to minister is greater than the need of the person being ministered to. This is unhealthy, subtle, and creates significant damage to ministry recipients. This temptation is insidious but widespread; it creeps up almost unnoticed, and before you realise what's happening you find yourself trapped.

Our personal fulfilment must come from who we are, not what 'gift' we are experienced in. Gifts are not a sign of maturity, just of God's grace. Ministering because we have the need to is not what is needed folks.

Ministry: It is a privilege to minster in God's name, to bless others, and to represent Jesus on earth. The 'successes' of any ministry are not measured by the results but the motives. When the motive is pure then God is honoured. Anyone who ministers is merely a waiter carrying what the chef has prepared to the diner who needs to 'digest' it.

Be acutely aware of the traps of pride, arrogance, and reputation-seeking, and cultivate humility, compassion, and love. Past practice in ministry, especially in a church context, must be displaced by a new spirit and heart that reflects who God is and not who the one ministering is.

Consider:

Can you check out your motives in ministry honestly?

Do you derive too much personal kudos from your ministry?

Ask Holy Spirit if you are seeing the true picture or not.

15 Distinguish between the written and the Living Word

The written word: The Bible is an amazing and inspired help for those who follow Jesus. However, much of what we choose to believe it says is, in fact, somebody's interpretation or opinion. There isn't life in the book unless revelation unpacks and explains what's being conveyed.

An intellectual grasp of scripture is not the same as a relationship with its author.

It is also true to say that English language translations are flawed by partial, misleading, or inadequate words.

Many confuse or merge the written word with the Living Word and give them equal importance, which is a poor choice (it can even be idolatrous).

The Living Word: The person (and example) of Jesus must be pre-eminent and not be in competition with any doctrinal conviction. Jesus is alive; He interacts with us in so many ways and lives in us by His Spirit. Let our spirit, which is attuned to Holy Spirit, form, inform, and reform our beliefs rather than a mind full of knowledge or opinions. Personal revelation is available to every believer and will be aligned with God's heart and purpose. The Bible explains some things (not everything), but life, mystery, encounter, and maturity are birthed and nurtured from experiential relationship.

Consider:

Is your reliance on the Bible greater than your reliance on your relationship with God?

Does your relationship with Holy Spirit shape your perception of what the Bible says, or does your theology define the nature of that relationship?

16 Distinguish between a church and the Church

A church: It's sad but vital that we don't confuse these two things – contrary to some people's opinion, they are not the same thing at all. Most local churches, not to mention denominations and national groups, streams, and networks, are man-made organisations and structures, and whilst there is much to be applauded and valued in them, they limit and restrict kingdom expression and activity. The problems of hierarchy, control, and rule-keeping thwart what God is seeking to release – loving, authentic, organic, responsive, spirit-led 'ecclesia'.

The Church: This is the expression of his kingdom freed from human constraint. It's radical, passionate, loving, united, kind, supernatural, creative, tender, meek, and reflects the glory and heart of God. Some of this can be found in a church – but not much. God is quietly extracting His Church, one person at a time, from their religious prison. It's a hidden and unnoticed family who will steward the harvest, welcome the prodigals, and walk in a power that's birthed and honed from revelation, dependence, brokenness, and humility.

Let's be clear, **our loyalty is to Jesus and His Church,** rather than anything or anyone else. He is our 'covering' and loving 'leader, and we joyfully, willing surrender to a life entwined with Him. We need to be wise and careful what or who else we yield to.

Consider:

Do you feel trapped, disillusioned, lost in a local church?

Do you confuse or merge a church with 'the' Church?

To whom or to what are you primarily loyal?

17 Distinguish between recruitment and love

Recruitment: For decades we have mistakenly believed that the commission Jesus gave us was to recruit others into the church. Evangelistic programmes, street preaching, sharing the good news, witnessing at work, haranguing sinners, and coming from a 'turn or burn' mindset and vocabulary really need to be consigned to history. The problem here is the heart motive, which rarely has love for the person but is keen to show people the error of their ways! Surely, this is not the example set by Jesus – the one who we follow and represent but rather seems more reminiscent of the Pharisees.

Love: Let's introduce people to Jesus (the person) rather than trying to 'convert' them. Reach out and represent Jesus to them because of the love in your heart, rather than any other motive. We are called to 'draw' not 'drive' people towards a real encounter with Jesus. What matters is that people 'see' something of the heart of God by meeting us rather than feeling the 'weight' of religious law. There was an endearing appeal about Jesus to many (not all!), and those who follow Him can exude the same because Holy Spirit resides in them. If we are harsh, unkind, judgemental, or arrogant in our interaction with others, it's not God's heart we exhibit, it's not love! Any gifting or anointing is hollow without love.

Consider:

Be honest.

Ask Holy Spirit to show you what heart motives you have.

Is your manner one characterised by correction or love?

How do you view those who are marginalised or 'different'?

Is 'you can't love others if you don't love yourself' an issue?

18 Distinguish between training and innate gifting

Training: I'm not suggesting that study and training are in themselves ungodly or unhelpful, just that they are confused with spiritual maturity. While ever they serve and enhance our relationship with Father, Jesus, and Holy Spirit, there is potential benefit and contribution. The problem comes when they obstruct or replace our spirit-to-Spirit relationship. This is why we need to know which is which and be able to perceive when their impact is negative or delusional. We can be efficient in applying biblical knowledge yet have an absence of relational reality. Let's not confuse academic qualifications, doctrinal expertise, or scriptural prowess with who we innately were created to be.

Innate gifting: Not only were we created to live at a specific time in history, but we were also impregnated with an innate and unique expression of divine DNA at our core. This is our personal expression of 'being made in the image of God'. It is utterly different from acquired knowledge and gifting, but they can partner together to great effect. When we live and function out of who we are innately, there is joy, fulfilment, and peace that can't be discovered and enjoyed any other way. Holy Spirit stands ready to reveal this to those who are unaware of who they are – just ask.

Consider:

What is your unique personal expression of divine DNA?

What makes you come alive in your spirit?

Do you rely too heavily on your training and 'expertise'?

Do you long for a life that is fulfilled and contented?

Has your theology boxed you in or set you free?

19 Distinguish between fragility and vulnerability

Fragility: This has the meaning of something, or someone, being brittle, weak, frail, or easily broken. There is a need for great care to be taken to avoid causing damage or worse. We avoid risk, pressure, stress, and movement for fear of a negative impact. Whilst this can be true of things and people physically, it's not a state or condition we should find or tolerate in ourselves spiritually. The security that comes from an intimate relationship with God ensures that even if we feel weak we don't have to live in a place of fragility.

Vulnerability: Many think that vulnerability is the same as fragility, but there are big differences that have ramifications.

In mature vulnerability, there is a strength that supports sensitiveness, accessibility, openness, and challenge without the fear or danger of breakage or damage.

Boundaries are still required, but being 'vulnerable' to others is a great gift and blessing that facilitates unity of the Spirit.

Transparency with love is transformative.

No more people on pedestals!

How amazing would it be to have leaders who are vulnerable yet secure and mature in their relationship with God.

It's wonderful to enjoy kindred spirit fellowship with others, 'vulnerably' and in the absence of control.

Consider:

Are you fragile – emotionally, mentally, spiritually? Why?

What helpful boundaries do you have in place?

What unhelpful boundaries do you have in place?

Are you secure enough in God to be vulnerable to others?

Do our past, unhealed wounds affect our present?

20 Distinguish between gifting and maturity

Gifting: Probably because we live in a world that places great store on qualification, expertise, and reputation, we often mistake these things for maturity. We make the same mistake with 'ministry' and think spiritual gifts equate to spiritual maturity – which is often not the case. Being known for our gifting says nothing about our character; having a title or reputation doesn't reveal who we are, just what we do. Spiritual gifts are just that – something God bestows as a free and unmerited present to us. It's not a sign of maturity!

Maturity: For us to exercise effectively any spiritual gift that we have for the benefit of others requires an ever-increasing degree of maturity. Being prophetic is amazing, but it needs to be partnered with wisdom. Having the eloquence to tell others the good news is great, but it needs to be birthed in love, not judgement. Intercession is needed but only effective if coupled with discernment. Gifts of the spirit are most effective when the fruit of the Spirit shapes and accompanies them. It's the **mature** children of God who respond to the impulses of Holy Spirit (Romans 8:14). Dominance of another, harsh speech, a critical mindset, not listening, spiritual pride and aloofness, pushy managerial leadership, or unkind insensitivity may be found in someone with gifting but will be largely absent in someone who is mature.

Consider:

Do you gauge spiritual maturity by Spirit 'gifts' or 'fruits'?

Is your gifting encased in love, wisdom, and honour?

Would you consider yourself to be mature in spirit?

21 Distinguish between servant and 'son'

Servant: Most of us understand that following Jesus and His example on earth means we are to be 'servant-hearted', not selfish, unkind, or mean. However, this doesn't mean that we are 'servants' or slaves. Our status in the kingdom of God is not that of someone enslaved by a master but that of a royal son or daughter whose father is the King of all kings. It is not our 'service' that honours God but our love and devotion to Him. If we think, speak, act, and believe that we are servants rather than 'sons', we relegate our heritage, authority, and position in God. We have free will and therefore choice as to whether we feel pressured/put upon by God like a servant or whether we enjoy the favour of Father, the love of our brother Jesus, and the friendship of Holy Spirit.

Son: Spiritually speaking, sonship is 'gender blind', so both male and female are included when that word is used in the Bible (in the context of Jewish culture).

Upon maturity, the father would give his son his authority to represent him; he would declare him to be a beloved 'son' with whom he was pleased! We now enjoy being royal children who inherit from our heavenly Father, who are married to Jesus the Son, and who are empowered by Holy Spirit.

Let's be more like sons and less like servants!

Remember there is no room for arrogance, pride, superiority, or judgement in 'sonship', as it's all by God's grace.

Consider:

Do you think, speak, and act like a royal 'son' or a servant?

Have you known God call you the 'apple of His eye'?

Do you experience the security that comes from 'sonship'?

22 Distinguish between enforced and voluntary

Enforced: This carries the connotation of coercion, compulsion, pressure, obligation, and rule-keeping. It's pretty much the opposite of voluntary. Forcing or demanding that someone does something you want is very rarely justifiable or appropriate. As an employer, parent, teacher, legislator, boss, or church leader, life is easier, more effective, and less stressful if others happily and willingly volunteer to engage and contribute. Organisational and hierarchical structures find it almost impossible to facilitate this, as it requires a more organic, flexible, peer-led approach.

Control and order by imposition has no place in the family of God, so why has it been prevalent for so long?

Voluntary: Loving and responding to God, loving others, and being kind because we choose to is vastly different from doing those things out of duty, obligation, or because its demanded and expected. There's such joy in interacting with God and others, in 'serving' others, and of living in godly community voluntarily – because it's our heart choice.

Leaders and influencers (church ones in particular) who refuse to 'enforce' are a precious and rare gift.

Ever seen a murmuration of starlings or a shoal of fish?

Unity and momentum without dominance or control.

Consider:

What do you do that's out of obligation to God or others? Why?

What do you obligate others to do? Why?

What makes your heart sing?

23 Distinguish between remorse and repentance

Remorse: I suspect that you already know that these two things are not the same. But we often forget to discern the difference, especially in ourselves. Feeling remorse, regret, guilt, shame, callous or conscience-stricken is horrible and bad for our health, but despite this it's possible to bury, ignore, bottle, or supress these feelings and 'move on'.

When this happens, there is a distinct possibility that we will repeat a previous scenario, damage others, and go through those feelings again. So really nothing changes, at least not permanently. Judas Iscariot was remorseful, but he wasn't repentant.

Repentance: Although this may look similar to remorse externally, it's a very different story internally. The heart is not so much guilt ridden as sad that we hurt the One we love. An essential element in repentance is a turning around to face the opposite direction so as not to repeat the same mistake. Repentance alters our thought life, our words, and our behaviour; remorse rarely, if ever, does that.

When we are deeply in love with God, it's easier not to do things that require repentance – the love motive is powerful. Rather than struggle and strive to change habits or get trapped in a cycle of guilt and shame, search for greater intimacy with Father, Jesus, and Holy Spirit.

Consider:

Have you ever muddled these two things in your own life?

Is there any situation where you need to replace passive remorse with active repentance?

Have you intentionally left something personal, unresolved?

24 Distinguish between hanging on and hope

Hanging on: Over the last 40 years, but especially since 2020, I have encountered many believers who are so fearful or disillusioned that they've developed a 'siege' mentality. 'I'm just hanging on for Jesus to return'. There's a streak of fatalism that runs through this negative mindset and that breeds greater fear and hopelessness – the antithesis of who Jesus calls us to be. We have been put here to influence the world and infect it with the glory and presence of God.

There really is no place for us to have a grin-and-bear-it outlook while we wait for God to 'extract us' from earth.

Hope: When we 'hope for the best' whilst secretly wondering if it will, faith is absent. Powerful, authentic, convinced hope is birthed in our relationship with God and our experience of who He is, not in our knowledge of the Bible. This blend of hope and faith, born out of who we know, is transformative for us and for others around us. It thrives despite circumstances and in the face of the seemingly impossible. It brings us a strong sense of security, confidence, and peace, which is pervasive even if we feel weak because it derives solely from our complete dependence on God. This hope is not outcome based but relational and unshakeable. Hanging on seems such a miserable and depressing state of mind in comparison!

Consider:

Are you full of faith-fuelled hope or just hanging on?

Do you think God has given up on earth and its inhabitants?

Is your expectation one of 'the glory of God' being seen?

Are you here to 'win the world' or 'escape the earth'?

25 Distinguish between pleading and declaring

Pleading: This distinction is in the context of praying, intercession, petition, and spiritual warfare. Prayer is a two-way communication process where we listen more than we talk, which enables us to know better what is currently in God's heart and to pray in alignment with that. Many have drifted to a place where they mainly talk to God when they have a need or an issue that they need Him to solve. Intercession has often involved a kind of pleading, almost begging vocabulary as we try to persuade God to help us or intervene in a situation. This isn't the posture of a child of the King. Yes, He is to be revered, but He's our 'Abba'.

Declaring: Providing we are in a healthy and meaningful personal relationship with God (not the caveat please), then we are empowered to speak on His behalf. Increasingly, I find that when I ask God to do something He replies by saying, 'Why are you asking Me when I've empowered you to do that?' or 'I have something more important to show or ask you so that will need to wait for another time'.

If we are entwined with the Three, we are authorised to speak into, and declare over, situations with the full expectation of our words making the difference. Find some relevant scriptures to declare and trust Holy Spirit for words.

Consider:

Do you know what authority you have been given by God?

Can you jettison a 'shopping list' view of prayer?

Declaration is powerful – are you engaged with that?

Ask Holy Spirit for fresh revelation in the area of prayer.

26 Distinguish between income and impact

Income: This comparison my seem a little left field, but it's time to re-evaluate what really matters in life. It is engrained in many of us that we must prioritise 'income'/money in order to thrive and enjoy life, and so it becomes a huge factor in how we think and behave. Whilst a good income, career, or lifestyle is laudable, they are **only destiny fulfilling if they facilitate our ability and opportunity to be the person we were created to be.** Our eternal legacy is not the material wealth or possessions we leave behind.

(N.B. There are some who God created to steward wealth.)

Impact: Each of us is born in God's specific time to fulfil the purpose we are given. The core focus of our life is to know who we are in order to execute the destiny God planned. This is when we can truly impact and influence our world for the glory of God. The personal fulfilment that comes from this is off the chart! It's joyful not stressful, fun not fraught.

Income passes away at death, but impact does not.

Our eternal legacy is the things and the people that were positively impacted as we lived in union with our Creator and His plan for us.

You are here to make an impact, not just an income!

Consider:

Are you motivated by a desire for income or impact?

Does your career choice allow you to be who God created?

What will your legacy be?

How can we live without a mindset of primary dependence on money?

When does responsibility give way to faith?

27 Distinguish between 'their' issues and your issues

Their issues: Our mental, emotional, and spiritual health are all affected by what we take on board. When others offend, hurt, belittle, ignore, or slander us, it can wound us if we allow it to. I wrestled for ages trying not to absorb other people's issues and problems, which then created issues or problems for me. I would take umbrage at negative things said to me, even respond harshly to 'give as good as I got'. The revelation that made the dramatic difference was when I realised that their unjust or offensive words were the result and expression of *their* wounds and hurts, rather than an attack on me (which is what it felt like). When we no longer have the need to defend ourselves, self-justify, or correct others, we are free of so much angst and pain.

Recognise that usually it's *their* issue not yours.

Your issues: When you are negatively impacted by others, rather than condemning, arguing, or reprimanding them, switch your focus from their input to why it adversely affects you. We are responsible for ourselves and our attitude but not responsible for anyone else's. Ask why did it hurt, upset, offend, or outrage you? What is it in you that needs healing to stop that reaction recurring? What button did it press?

If we focus on 'our issues', two things happen; one, 'their issues' become much less of a trigger and problem, and two, we mature and become more like Jesus!

Consider:

How can you focus less on their issues and more on yours?

What issues in your past are you still carrying?

Do you respond or react to people and situations?

28 Distinguish between quitting and resting

Quitting: This distinction is understood by few. Stopping activity can be giving up, which is a negative choice, usually born out of frustration, disappointment, disillusion, or pique. Living at too fast a pace of life can bring burnout and breakdown where a person just crashes and quits. We need regular space and pause to avoid this horrid place of having to quit.

Resting: It is too easy to view resting as quitting. However, building rest into our lifestyle is wise, healthy, godly, and transformative, yet many are too driven to implement it.

We were created to enjoy and benefit from 'rest'; it's in our DNA, and we ignore to our detriment. 'Be still and know' is scriptural advice. We are unlikely to hear God's 'still small voice' without establishing a pattern of rest. The Bible speaks a lot about rest and how God leads us there, so we do well to heed and explore what that means for us personally. Having the principle of rest in our lives enables us to 'wait' on, and for, God. This kind of rest is not passive, sitting in a vacuum, twiddling our thumbs; no, it's a place of love, reassurance, peace, patience, and enjoyment. It makes a massive difference to our lives and our health.

Consider:

Is rest a part of your life and spiritual discipline?

Are you too busy to adopt a pattern and rhythm of physical, mental, emotional, and spiritual rest?

How could you practically improve your level of rest?

Do you know how to wait on God patiently (no gritted teeth).

Explore meditating with God, silence, nature, and relaxation.

29 Distinguish between busyness and effectiveness

Busyness: We live in a frenetic world, people rushing around at breakneck speed, and communication that demands an instant response. People are living under pressure on so many levels. Yet we were not created to live like that; we are out of sync with our Creator and how He designed us to function. Spiritual health and growth can't thrive in this environment. Revelation rarely comes to the busy.

God is asking us to 'ruthlessly eliminate hurry' as a priority.

Busyness is very rarely a mark of effectiveness.

Effectiveness: It needs an eternal perspective to truly measure whether we are being effective in regard to our calling and purpose. What the world highly values and what God highly values have very little overlap. We are learning to measure effectiveness by how we honour God, how we love other people – our attitude, love, kindness, and compassion – not our theology!

Please be so careful, especially in ministry, not to count level of output, activity, successes, converts, programmes, or even numbers as the yardstick to determine effectiveness. Fulfilling our destiny by being who we were made to be is the most likely path to being an effective child of God.

Slow down!

Consider:

Do you call yourself a 'doer' who needs to be constantly on the go?

Does being really busy make you feel better?

Are you avoiding facing up to something by being too busy?

How do you measure your own 'effectiveness'?

Do you need to rethink the balance and rhythm of your life?

30 Distinguish between an earthly and a heavenly perspective

Earthly perspective: In every situation, circumstance, relationship, thought, feeling, trial, problem, and challenge, we have the choice to employ one of two perspectives, the physical or the spiritual, the human or the godly, the finite or the eternal. Which is our dominant everyday reality?

Looking at anything from an earthly point of view, we will take more notice of the situation than who god is. Our issue will colour and dominate the spiritual reality, and we tend to then see God through our problem rather than seeing the problem through our heart knowledge of who God is.

Perspective is a choice we make.

Heavenly perspective: The key to having this view is to allow the voice of your spirit to speak louder than your mind, body, or soul. The facts facing us remain unchanged, but our view of it, and therefore our response to it, will depend on our choice of perspective. Let God be the 'foreground' of our life's picture and everything else be the 'background. Our focus will have a massive consequence to how we journey through life. Often what we consider in the natural to be a negative scenario are things that when looked at in the spiritual God utilises to redirect or mature us. This can help us to embrace pain, change, loss, rejection, and disappointment.

It's profound!

Consider:

Which perspective do you usually choose?

Which do we give greater credence to, the 'facts' or God's heart and character?

Which reality do you start from, earth's or heaven's?

POSTSCRIPT

If, as I suspect, you have been 'triggered' by something you've read and had an emotional, mental, or spiritual reaction, I have a respectful request; instead of being upset, angry, or offended, pause and ask Holy Spirit why you had that particular response in regard to that statement.

....

....

Was the reaction in your head, your feelings, or your spirit?

....

What was it specifically that you reacted to?

....

....

What 'button' does it press?

....

What does it say about you (positive or negative)?

....

....

....

This is not a time to quibble over doctrine or interpretation as we prepare for what lies ahead.

Let's ensure that the enemy can have no voice among us.

We are all on a steep learning curve which requires us to 'unlearn' much in order to embrace fresh and personal revelation from God himself.

Shalom.

Discernment has become a necessity rather than an option. Only intimate familiarity with the authentic enables the effective recognition of the counterfeit.

UNCHARTED

Are you aware that we are living at a pivotal moment in history, both as inhabitants of earth and as followers of Jesus?

Do you know what the future looks like? It's imperative that we perceive the season and time in which we live in order to be aligned with what God is doing in our world and His kingdom. This book contains handy hints and tell-tale hallmarks to help the journey of transition.